The Joy of Progressive Dinners
A Gourmet Guide to Friendmaking

The Joy of Progressive Dinners

A Gourmet Guide
to Friendmaking

WRITTEN BY
Gab Cody and Sam Turich

EDITED BY
Gab Cody, Charlie Kasov and Sam Turich

ILLUSTRATIONS BY
Mary M. Mazziotti

APPENDIX ILLUSTRATIONS BY
Nicole Antonuccio

DESIGN, COVER AND LAYOUT BY
Jennifer Navari

Special thanks to
Jasdeep Khaira and Cynthia Pearson

progressionmovie.com
progressionfilm@gmail.com

ISBN: 978-1540516190

To the cast, crew and supporters of the feature film
Progression, for teaching us about friendship.

"Your lies are wilting the arugula."

Contents

Preface

Welcome, New Friend:

You seem to have found yourself reading the preface for *The Joy of Progressive Dinners: A Gourmet Guide to Friendmaking*. How did you get here? What questionable life decisions have brought you to this moment? We don't know, but you're here now, so let's make the best of it. Sit down, grab a beverage that supports your life goals, and prepare to learn how to throw your very own progressive dinner.

You have a few questions. Let's tackle the obvious one first: What's with the title of this book?

Long, long ago in the Before Times, back when people couldn't satisfy their fleshy urges at the touch of a button [read: no "Tinder" no "Grindr" no "Blendr"], Dr. Alex Comfort and a team of illustrators took it upon themselves to create a book called *The Joy of Sex: The Gourmet Guide to Lovemaking*. The authors were riffing on *The Joy of Cooking*, which is a cookbook that everyone knows.

When we were kids, *The Joy of Sex* was everywhere. It was translated into more than 20 languages, and sold more than 10 million copies. It was on *The New York Times* best-seller list for a decade. And who knows, maybe people ACTUAL-LY used it as a sex guide. We haven't found anyone willing to ask their parents about it... yet.

If you want to enjoy our guide to friend-making on multiple levels, check out the original and then look for our moments of overt tribute. But be forewarned, *JOS* is not for the faint of heart. Do not look at it while at work or in the company of your parents. It's filled with these... drawings. Pen-and-ink, quasi-classy, not-at-all-sexy but super graphic depictions of sex play, drawn, it can now be told, from life. Not just any life, but the life of the hairy, bearded illustrator, Charles Raymond and his hairy German wife, Edeltraud. This was before manscaping. Before bush trimming. Apparently before armpit shaving. By 21st-century standards, it's a goddamn trainwreck. YOU HAVE BEEN WARNED.

Now here we are, contributing a tongue-in-cheek (see *The Joy of Sex*, Chapter 3) homage to both books (the sex book and the cookbook) and delivering unto you – and your friends, and anyone from Pittsburgh, and anyone who wants to start their own progressive dinner, and anyone who en-joys being amused through reading – an entirely new book: part instruction manual, part life lesson, part cookbook. (With drawings!) This is not a sex manual. If you need a sex manual, we will write one for you for $200,000. No checks.

Okay, question two: Why a cookbook about how to throw a progressive dinner?

The short answer: Because we made a movie set at a progressive dinner called *Progression*. (FREE copy with this book.)

Longer Answer:

It all began when we ran, hair on fire, out of Brooklyn to a city where it's possible to sleep, eat and make art. That city is Pittsburgh. (Don't move here. We like it the way it is. Unless you're a person of color or someone who's going to open an amazingly delicious food truck. If you are a POC or a FTO[1], we'll leave the light on for you, please move here. If you're someone thinking about moving back, well, obviously, we can't stop yinz.)

When we arrived, we decamped to a neighborhood called Lawrenceville. We liked Lawrenceville because it looks like Brooklyn, is littered with old industrial sites and, the clincher, the night we moved into our rental rowhouse (you can rent a WHOLE house??) we witnessed the one-and-only car fire we've ever seen here. Its smoldering rubber and fiberglass parts offered an olfactory transition between old and new. Take that, Bushwick.

Within a month of moving to the neighborhood, we were invited to the annual Lawrenceville Urban Pioneer Society Progressive Dinner. It's an annual event (running 30 years now) where more than 150 neighbors, split into groups of about 10, share three courses at different homes, all in one night.

Wouldn't that be a funny premise for a movie? we thought. Yes, we answered ourselves. Should we try to find some famous people to be in our movie and some famous people to make the movie? Nah! This is Pittsburgh, man, we're underdogs! We're going to do this in the most authentic, most interesting way that no one will ever find out about. We're

---

[1] Food Truck Operator

going to make an independent comedy feature, set at a progressive dinner, just like the one in our neighborhood. We'll call it *Progression*. (FREE copy with this book!)

What's that? You just checked out our hand-drawn, quirkily disarming website, progressionmovie.com, and you're asking question number three: "Is this a charming PG-13 experience about community-building that the entire family will enjoy?"

No.

Just don't.

Like the actual progressive dinner in our neighborhood, this film is for adults only. Though the film is not yet rated, it'd be rated R for brief male nudity, sexual situations, adult language throughout, comic violence, and kielbasa.

So put the kiddies to bed before you pop the movie in. Okay?

And remember as you're watching, for a micro-budget feature like this one, our neighbors helped by donating locations for filming, acting as extras, preparing meals for the cast and crew, and cheering the whole team on. We shot the whole movie right here in the neighborhood.

So get ready to take part in a community event.

Visit our website, progressionmovie.com, for more information on the film and to learn how to eventually watch it online. (Did we mention you get a FREE copy of the film with this book? Lucky you!)

It's lovely to meet you. Let's do this again.

Truly yours in friendship,
Gab Cody & Sam Turich

On Advanced Friendmaking

Remember that time that never existed when everyone in America got along? Using *The Joy of Progressive Dinners: A Gourmet Guide to Friendmaking*, you can revive Imaginary America, build real community and get to know your neighbors well enough to give salient answers to the police.

This book is not just a cookbook. A cookbook tells the novice how to tackle a live lobster, what to do when the mayonnaise separates, how to fix a chateaubriand. This book will tell the novice friend-maker how to tackle a boor, how to seat a couple who have separated, how to fix it when you arrive with domestic beer at "Chateau Brian's."

To use this book, the first thing you need to accept is this: It's not your fault. It's not your fault you don't know all your neighbors, or have friends up and down your street like they did back in Imaginary America. A Pew Social & Demographic Trends survey finds that, "Most Americans have moved to a new community at least once in their lives… Asked why they lived where they do, movers most often cite the pull of economic opportunity. "

So you moved, maybe for a job, and transitioning to the new workplace took up most of your potential friend-making time. Or maybe you're part of a demographic that faces other demands on your freedom to make new friends. As our lives transition from family to school, then to university or job, then to adult friendships and then back to marriage and family, our friend-making follows a bell curve. In the middle, we make a lot of friends while we're at school and starting adulthood, but at the ends of the curve, not so much. You can't make many friends when you're crib-bound. And at the other end, it's tough to get familiar with folks when parenting, the recognized truth being that friendships are formed through shared time, shared experiences and not so much at 9pm on a school night when someone forgot she had a science report due the next day.

Although humans used to live in multigenerational tribes, in the 21st century we find intermingling across age groups and demographics is typically reserved for family affairs. But if you're interested in building community, you're going to have to make friends with curmudgeons (old farts), 20-year-old internet billionaires (new farts) as well as middle-aged artists and artisans (smelly farts).

If you're a beginner at friend-making, knowing your neighbors and your community will enrich your life. There's not a better way to get to know the folks who live in your neighborhood than by attending a progressive dinner.

And using this book, starting your own progressive dinner has never been simpler.

This being a Pittsburgh book, we also provide a special FAQ to tackle local Pittsburgh problems such as: the parking chair, car-keying and topics of conversation to avoid if you're not on the vegan track (hint: bicycles).

If you're not in Pittsburgh, we encourage you to create your own local FAQ, which should include everything ridiculous, annoying, stupid – but seemingly inescapable – in your neighborhood.

What follows is a step-by-step guide to arranging your own progressive dinner for your community and in doing so, making new friends (who all live right nearby). We'll break down the logistics for you, offer expert tips and share recipes for any occasion. It's going to be a little bit naughty, just like *Progression* and *The Joy of Sex*.

Bon Appétit et Belles Amitiées!

So, you're probably wondering, "What the hell is a progressive dinner?!" Well, stop that uncalled-for cussing and get some knowledge.

Starters

pro·gres·sive din·ner

noun
a social occasion at which the different courses of a meal are eaten at different people's homes.

Note that this is not the same as a "Progressive's dinner" (kale) or "Progressives' dinner" (extra kale, with a side of micro-greens-aggression).

A progressive dinner is a meal that takes place over the course of an evening at multiple locations. If you're new to this, you might consider starting by organizing a progressive dinner for 10 or 12 diners at three locations. Once you're more experienced (or sooner, if you're adventurous), you can grow your dinner all the way up to a community-wide event like the one we have in Lawrenceville, 150 diners at 50 neighbors' homes.

The important thing is that you move your body, shake your groove thing and break bread with as many of your neighbors as you can.

tables

Still the most important piece of domestic dining equipment. But don't worry if you don't have one. Some of the most exciting and memorable meals of a person's life take place in unusual locations – the back of the car, in a public place or even on an airplane. Remember that the essential idea of a progressive dinner is to invite people into your home, table or no table. If your home is under construction and your guests must eat TV dinners off of moving boxes, call it ironic-redneck-retro or how-the-99-percent-lives and just enjoy yourself.

Friendmaking is best enjoyed when you can be yourself. You show them yours, and they will show you theirs. It's not the size of the table that makes a winner of the dinner.

birdsong at morning

Everyone has particular tastes. Some of us are turkeys, and we enjoy jib-jabbering and gobble, gobble, gobble. Some of us are bowerbirds – intricate, artful constructors of new realities drawn from our current situations. And some of us are peacocks, strutting, preening and honking loudly for attention. In the end, as long as we accept we're all fowl in one way or another we can respect each other's tastes. Your meal won't please everyone. Don't take it personally. Your personality won't please everyone. Don't take it personally.

You know "The 4 Agreements" your homemade-kombucha-sipping friend is always going on about? Best bone up on them before you open your home to a bunch of strangers who live right up the street.

nakedness

Not recommended. Either off-putting or too inviting. Exposing your two bits can get you into trouble, and sharing your two cents may likewise discomfit your new friends.

Should you keep your truth under wraps? Like flavorless pudding, a person without opinions will be the most palatable to the most people. Stronger opinions, like stronger spices, will narrow your appeal but create a more profound reaction.

It is the opinion of the authors that it is better to be the Freak-Flag-Fly-in-the-ointment rather than a Paragon of Pablum.

Pab·lum
noun
A processed cereal for infants originally marketed by the Mead Johnson Company in 1931. The trademarked name is a contracted form of the Latin word pabulum, which means "foodstuff."

That said, these are your neighbors: you will see these folks again. But if you can't be yourself in your own home, then you might want to look into building a safe room where you can just say whatever you want. Or just go on the Internet.

virginity

You might be a progressive dinner virgin yourself or you might be hosting progressive dinner virgins. In either case, remember there's a first time for everything. In this case we do not suggest closing your eyes and thinking of England, but rather opening your heart and remembering that your prime directive is friendmaking. Take your time. Whatever you do, be gentle and slow. And don't skimp on the lubricant (see "relaxation").

relaxation

Most of the stops on your progressive dinner journey will include wine or other alcoholic beverages. These might be provided by the host or by the guests, depending on how you organize your event (we suggest the hosts provide the beverages).

Just remember, you're starting with a new glass at each house. When we polled progressive dinner participants, one of the most important pieces of advice we received was: Pace Yourself. If you drink too much at one dinner party, you're embarrassed. If you drink too much at two dinner parties, you've got a problem. If you drink too much at three dinner parties that all oc-

cur in the space of two hours, you've bought a one-way ticket to Barftown on the Puking-in-the-Planters Express.

Whether you're drinking or not, meeting new people and making friends can be exciting (extrovert) or life-threateningly harrowing (introvert). Just remember: relaxation is key. In the words of the immortal Bill Murray:

You have to remind yourself that you can do the very best you can when you're very, very relaxed, no matter what it is, whatever your job is. The more relaxed you are, the better you are.

Your job is friend-making. Be relaxed and get to it.

size

Preoccupation with the size of your table is "neurotic in the good way." Some people have tables so big it's painful. Other people have smaller tables, which they use to great advantage. But don't obsess about the table and then forget about the chairs. Think carefully about how many people you can please at the same time. Determining what you can handle will allow you to challenge yourself without disappointing your poor, hungry guests.

Look at your table. Count your chairs. Consider your time. Aim a little lower than you can handle and increase the size if the organizers need extra spots. In this way you don't overstretch yourself and you also endear yourself to those volunteer organizers when there's an emergency and another host cancels (pro tip: this will happen).

If you're the organizer, share the above with each of your hosts so they know not to take too much at once.

"One time our beloved dog Zena ate
the meatballs from the kitchen counter
5 minutes before I was leaving for the
appetizer course. I did what any other
Italian woman would do, and that was
'call daddy.' My dad promptly went to
the Italian store in Bloomfield and bought
readymade meatballs."
— Catherine Lafferty, LUPS veteran

Main
Courses

Some may think that you can get too old to enjoy progressive dinners, that it's natural to lose your interest in friendmaking. Others believe that you can be too young, and your inexperienced penetrations will only chafe the delicate surfaces of your neighbors' interiors.

But an experienced hand can gently redirect the passion of youth to even greater heights of intercourse. And raw ardor can reacquaint the hardened campaigner of the softer surfaces that linger still inside.

A good progressive dinner brings together lots of different types of people. Old timers and newbies, seniors and newlyweds, great grandparents and folks with babies in slings. All ready to share their passion, their energy and their complaints about parking.

NOTE: Our progressive dinner does not allow children. Nursing babies in slings: OK. Toddlers running around terrorizing the host's preternaturally aloof Siamese cat: Not OK. This is not because progressive dinner people are against the perpetuation of the species (many hosts and guests are parents). This is because a progressive dinner is an adult event. An adult event where people can discuss politics, manscaping and violence without junior asking for clarification on that first marriage you never mentioned before.

Progressive dinners are great for learning things about your community that you'd never find out otherwise. If you've been there for years you'll hear all about what it's like to be new in town. If you've just moved in you'll find out what it was like to live there 50 years ago.

Possible things you'll learn about your neighborhood:

"It used to be so racist!"
"It's so much more racist!"
"No one cared about race as long as you were Catholic."

A progressive dinner is one of the best, most enjoyable ways we know to build a community in your neighborhood. There's something about breaking bread with people that allows folks to let their guard down, to speak freely and to discover common ground.

So how do you connect with your community, to get a progressive dinner started?

touching

Gently reach for your neighbors, being careful to first gain their consent. Slowly massage your contact list of interested neighbors. Languidly work your way toward social media: Facebook groups and other sites like Nextdoor (but not Tindr, Grindr, or Yinzr). If you're ready to invite new partners, entrust neighbors to tempt their contacts as well.

reach around

If you want to shoot your message all over, but you're more comfortable with something traditional, you may tenderly rendezvous with your neighbors in all the old school ways: talking to folks when you see them around the neighborhood, flyers in the local shops and on bulletin boards, phone trees, or ringing doorbells. Word-of-mouth may be your best tool for getting started. Examples of DIY neighborhood signage:

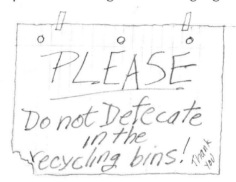

Once you've got your list, email is the easiest way to communicate with everyone, though online invitation sites or Facebook can also work. Email generally encompasses multiple generations, and it's easier to keep a list going from year to year.

If your dinner is a success and you want to make it a regular event, you'll need to manage the list, keeping it up to date and adding new names as more folks request invitations. We also recommend regularly passing the organizing duties along to other neighbors every year or two, so no one carries the burden for too long. Google Docs is a good way to share your progressive dinner contact list with multiple organizers. Just make sure to back it up regularly.

Remember to be safe online. Build bridges, watch out for trolls.

a hot date

What night is everyone in the mood? Is there ever a bad time for a progressive dinner? Saturdays are best, since usually you'll want to start things in the late afternoon (and leave everybody room to stay out late, if things are really hopping).

JOKE: What do you get when you cross a dog with a frog?

ANSWER: A dog that can lick itself from across the room.

Fridays can also work, but school nights can be tricky (see "relaxation"). Keep a wary eye on the calendar to avoid holiday weekends that might mean lots of neighbors will be out of town or otherwise engaged.

Our progressive dinner is always the second or third Saturday in October – that way we avoid Halloween and the other major holiday weekends, and Thanksgiving is far enough off that we don't feel like we've got to cook another big meal right away. Also, the weather is usually mild enough that traversing the neighborhood is easy.

Other good months are April and May (avoiding Easter, Passover, Mother's Day and Ramadan). Over the summer, dates that avoid the three-day weekends can work, but cooking in the heat can spoil the mood and a tableful of sweaty guests can be grumpy and smelly.

We recommend setting the date at least 2 months ahead of time, though more than that is even better. Send out a save-the-date email as soon as possible, then you can fill in details as the date gets closer. Making friends takes conscientious planning. We can't all meet cute in a Rob Reiner film.

who's coming?

You can set the number of diners ahead of time, or you can just wait to see how many folks want to participate. Limiting the geographical area is important, and you may set the borders however you like. Our dinner is limited to only people who live in our neighborhood (as defined by certain border streets that just about everybody in town agrees on).

Make sure there's room to park or, if possible, make your progressive dinner an on-foot affair. In Pittsburgh, people are very serious about the parking spots directly outside of their houses. They use technologically advanced mechanisms to ensure these spots remain open, e.g., the parking chair:

Remember that most folks can host 6-10 guests around their tables (and keep in mind that the hosts need a place to sit, too). When you're setting up the hosting, you'll want to make sure you know just how many guests each host can accommodate.

A long-time progressive dinner participant and our illustrator, Mary Mazziotti, offered us this advice from a homemaking book:

Whom to Invite: Great tact should be exercised in selecting guests for a dinner party. Those moving in the same social circle and known congeniality should be brought together. Religiously inclined persons would not be agreeably entertained by those inclined to theatricals or dancing.

— "Mrs. Owens' Cook Book and Useful Household Hints" 1884

The authors tend towards theatricals and dancing. One of the delights of a progressive dinner is the heterogeneity of guests who appear at your table. The organizers, beset by their guests' dietary restrictions and grudges old and new, will not always be able to arrange a table with as much care as Mrs. Owens. However, reaching out far and wide to diverse members of the community to formulate your guest pool will ensure your tables are interesting.

Based on our experience, the more people you involve overall the more challenging the organizing becomes. One cadre of 8-10 people is the easiest way to start a progressive dinner tradition (that's one group of diners visiting three homes). If you find 16-20 people who want to participate, you'll need six homes and hosts. A cadre of 24-30 will require 9 homes, and so on.

how much is too much?

Three courses (soup, salad, entrée) is ideal for organizational and time management purposes. Because our pool of participants is so large (sometimes more than 150 people!) we also hold an all-participant appetizer course to kick off the evening, and another all-participant dessert course at the end.

Of course, for these pre- and post-dinner events you'll need to find a location big enough to hold all the participants. We recommend finding a local gallery, restaurant or social club that's willing to host you for free for a few hours.

Asking entrepreneurs or real estate professionals who might be opening or marketing new locations is always a good bet – they'd love to have a bunch of their new neighbors find out all about their new place. The appetizer and dessert courses can easily be potluck and/or BYOB – as you've probably figured out from the math in the previous section, there are plenty of participants who AREN'T hosting a course at home (10 participants=5 couples, minus three hosted courses, leaving two couples to prepare appetizers and desserts).

amomaxia

Ever heard this word before? We hadn't either. We tried to think of a word that meant, "making love in a car," and realized to our surprise that there wasn't one. Except there is: amomaxia. Which technically is a clinical condition and/or fetish, but according to the Urban Dictionary is something almost every American of drinking age has tried at least once.

Anyway, one of the reasons a neighborhood is the perfect size for a progressive dinner is that you can walk everywhere the evening takes you. This becomes important when there is drinking involved (and there usually is) but it's also just a terrific way to feel more connected to the area you live in. It's not essential, however.

A progressive dinner staged over a wider area can bring together folks from adjacent neighborhoods, perhaps, or you could fashion a list of participants who share a particular interest (all the parents and teachers from an elementary school, say, or everybody in town who loves games). Though it's important to remember that the diversity of the participant list is part of what makes the experience so special.

It's also important to remember that, to keep the evening from going on for hours and hours, we schedule about an hour for each course. This means that diners have about 45 minutes in a house before it's time for everyone to leave and head to the next course, so that they all stay on schedule. Remember that at each soup and salad course you'll usually have at least one couple at your table that has to run home because they're hosting next. Limiting the geographical area of the dinner becomes an essential part of staying on schedule.

spread sheets

The virtual kind of sheets, not the ones you spread over your bed. So now you have a good list of folks who want to participate, and you've set a date. What's next?

First off, you'll need to check on dietary restrictions. That way you'll learn how many special tables you'll need to arrange for the evening. There are many online tools that can help you organize (googledocs, doodle, meetingwizard, etc.)

Then you need to know who is willing to host, what courses they're available for, whether they're willing to accommodate dietary restrictions, and how many guests they can seat comfortably at their table. Now is the time to identify the person most able to create, populate and manage a spreadsheet. Look for one of those Steve Urkel, Monica Geller, Mark Zuckerberg types. If you find the right person, maybe they'll make an algorithm for you or teach you how to solve that classic puzzle of combinatorics, "The Dinner Party Problem."

You'll want to remember the basic 5-course structure of the progressive dinner:

APPETIZERS (optional for progressive dinners with more than 12 total guests): Allow 30 minutes. Everyone convenes at a large location in the neighborhood. Those folks who are not hosting a course should help with setup, and provide the appetizers and beverages. All attendees pick up their Dance Cards. Their Dance

Card tells them where they are going for each course. It is an actual card. It does not necessarily feature the word "dance."

SOUP: Allow 1 total hour. Hosts should seat between 8-12 people.

SALAD: Allow 1 total hour. Hosts should seat between 8-12 people.

ENTRÉE: Allow 1 total hour. Hosts should seat between 8-12 people.

DESSERT: Those diners who are not hosting provide desserts and beverages. Choose a large establishment. A live local band and room for dancing is encouraged. At this point, if you disregarded our advice about imbibing responsibly, you can grab a neighbor and "dance it out" with abandon. (Pro tip: As you sweat out that Chablis, don't forget to rehydrate.) As Pittsburghers, it is our civic duty to recommend the Polka.

The easy thing to do is draw a DIAGRAM (see appendix) of host locations, with numbered slots for each location's guest capacity. Now, you begin the process of assigning participants to each course.

Once you have your diagram of host locations you can start filling in seats. We usually send our participants out as couples, so that's the algorithm we'll use. But you could try to send out singletons, or split couples up for the ultimate get-to-know-your-neighbors challenge.

This is the juncture when you must put on your Emily Post hat and diplomatically place diners in situations where they are least likely to encounter The Neighbor Who Tore Down My Tree or My Ex-Wife Who Left Me to Marry a Woman or My Brother Who Lives in the Neighborhood But I Refuse to Speak to Because of That Thing That Happened in '98. You can't possibly please everyone, but you can save your hosts all sorts of mishegas by being as nebby[2] as the cabal of citizens in *The Music Man* singing "Pick-A-Little, Talk-A-Little" or, for those with more literary tastes, Mrs. Bennet in *Pride and Prejudice*.

---

[2] nebby: Pittsburghese for nosey, i.e., "Sorry to be nebby, but how's come did yinz plant them flyers?"

doing the dance card

dance card
noun, dated
plural noun: dance cards
a card bearing the names of a woman's
prospective partners at a formal dance.
Used metaphorically in modern parlance.

Back when there were formal balls, young women would fill out cards to make sure they knew who their partners would be for each dance. While it took all of the spontaneity out of the affair, at least she'd know where she was going after every number.

We use the dance card (see appendix) in the same way. Each attendee or couple at the progressive dinner gets a card that tells them where to go for each course. It's handy, easy to read, and a nice keepsake after the event. Print 'em up, fill 'em out using your handy dandy DIAGRAM as your guide. Distribute them at the Appetizer course.

bondage & discipline

Who doesn't love rules? As the organizer, you must take a firm hand in establishing the strict regulations all diners must follow. We leave to your imagination the punishments with which you shall threaten transgressors. Pro tip: we do not recommend nipple clamps or ball gags.

Rules don't make you popular. Remember, friendship isn't all about warm feelings and birthdays on Facebook. *Psychology Today* sums it up:

> **There is a dark side to friendship. The people who know you the best are also the ones who have the most power to betray you...**

So put on your Dark Lord pants and enforce these non-negotiable rules:

1) Follow Your Dance Card

Everybody gets a "dance card" at the beginning of the night, which tells you where to go for each course. It's part of the fun to not know where you'll go until you're going there. ("I've always wondered who lived in that scary haunted house Victorian!")

☐ only go to the house you've been assigned.
☐ only bring the number of people who have signed up (each home has set exactly as many places at the table as are expected.)

☐ don't bring along an uninvited guest just because you think it'll be fun (you're not in this for the fun—you're here to make friends.)

And don't go to a house that's not on your dance card, even if you want to follow the hottie from Soup to the next course. It isn't meant to be, okay? And you can track that person down at dessert, anyway, and hopefully they didn't meet their soul mate at the Entree.

It's okay to skip a course, if there's an emergency, but when you attend a course you can only go where you've been assigned.

2) Welcome Your Guests

The authors are never sure which is more fun, hosting a course or visiting other folks' homes for theirs. Some people go to great lengths to lay out impressive spreads, others keep it simple. But the most important things are:

☐ you're ready at your appointed time.
☐ you've set out the correct number of places.
☐ you have enough of whatever you've made to go around.

Don't get angry at the vegans if they accidently end up at your house for beef stew. They're vegans – they're used to near-starving conditions. Offer them a mushroom broth and a carrot and a genuine smile.

Home cooking is always preferred, but sometimes neighbors have been known to "order in." It's not technically against the rules (we all know unexpected things can happen), but making yummy food for your neighbors can be one of the most satisfying parts of the progressive dinner.

Oh, and be prepared to offer something to drink – we usually provide both something non-alcoholic and wine and beer (as pairs well with the food).

3) Get A Move On

Keep an eye on the clock. Remember that you've all got to move along to the next course on time and on schedule. Chase folks away from your table if you have to. Be polite, but firm. Be gentle, this isn't a race.

a missive from a concerned citizen regarding oenophilia

So, you've decided to a host a course at a progressive dinner. One of the challenges of pairing wine with food is making sure that your guests are happy. However, they are getting free wine, so why should they complain? It can be stressful, having strangers in your home, meeting new people, making one of your favorite dishes hoping for validation. The proper balance of wine can make the evening playful, imaginative, pleasurable, exhilarating perhaps even erotic and passionate. Take control of your evening by making sure that you have the right wines. First, buy a bottle of your favorite wine for yourself, you deserve it, then hide the bottle within easy reach. Before the crowd arrives you may need a bit of 'Dutch Courage,' so consider a cocktail. I recommend a Classic Gin & Tonic, a Manhattan or a Martini. Sure, your guests may bring a bottle of wine with some obscure label they found in the clearance bin, but why subject yourself to that? If you are hosting a soup or salad course, opt for a lighter wine, like a Sauvignon Blanc, Red Blend or even a Sparkling Wine – like a Cava or Moscato. If you are braving it as a main course host, worry not. A Pinot Noir is a versatile wine that goes well with dishes from roast chicken to beef bourguignon. Finally, if you are hosting the dessert course consider offering a punch, it just takes 5 ingredients – alcohol, sweet, tart, fruity and spicy – use your imagination. Overall, relax and enjoy.

Cheers,
Raj Sabharwal, Wine & Spirits Importer and Certified Spirits Specialist

"I like making the salad, because it is less pressure than the main course and soup is just confusing to me as a starter. Soup IS dinner."
— Dana Gold

Sauces
& Pickles

à chacun son goût

We try to assign certain diners to "tracks" based on their dietary requirements – a series of host locations (soup-salad-entree) where their special needs can be met.

Here are the dietary proclivities of which we are currently aware: vegan, vegetarian, pescatarian, gluten free, lowcarb/atkins, raw food, hunter/gatherer, vampire, brains only, plus all other possible allergies. Your progressive dinner will quickly turn into *Night of the Living Dead* if you attempt to appease every diner.

The easiest way to divide your progressive dinner tracks without driving yourself into uncontrollable anger is thus:

1. All foods
2. Vegetarian/Vegan

You might separate vegetarian from vegan depending on your neighborhood preferences, or you might find you have the time, patience and ability to create a gluten-free, dairy-free or okra-free track.

o·kra
noun
a. a plant of the mallow family with long ridged seedpods, native to the Old World tropics.
b. The snottiest of all vegetables. Its mucilaginous attitude demands that it always be served with tissue.

arrival dysfunction

There will almost certainly be cancellations. Guests cancelling is manageable; hosts cancelling can be a nightmare. Plan for this in advance. It is well documented that preparation and planning can curb anxiety. Look on the Internet. And exercise more. Exercise is good for everyone and should be done a lot. Eat fruits and vegetables. Make sure you are getting enough sleep. Volunteer at a homeless shelter. Provide a scholarship to a bright kid who just needs a little encouragement. Consider whether access to healthcare is an entitlement or a basic right. What about water? Mull over whether your actions today contributed to pollution or ameliorated damage to the natural environment. Check your privilege and reconsider the disparities on which our country was built. And when a host cancels, remember which of your other hosts had extra space at their tables, because you were smart and didn't fill them to capacity, because you knew this day would come, you smartypants.

controlling size

You have the good kind of problem: It's too big! Your dinner is so popular! Everyone wants to go! How can you control the size of your progressive dinner, so it stays fun for you and everyone involved? Determine your optimal size and then create limits to attendance that will prevent things from getting out of control. Limits can be geographical, first-come/first-serve or odor-based. Our local dinner is limited to people who live in the neighborhood, and while people who live outside want to come, we simply don't let them. It's always a sad day when someone moves to another part of town, and can't come to the dinner anymore. But they have to live with their decision.

domination and submission

Share the responsibility for the organizing of your progressive dinner. See if you can convince a neighbor to help. Then, after you've done it for a few years, let that plucky young starlet **Eve**[3] give it a go. Sharing is caring.

naming your thing

Be careful. You don't want to sound like a gentrifying asshole. The name of our local dinner, which started out tongue-in-cheek but now makes us cringe a little, is LUPS, for "Lawrenceville Urban Pioneer Society." We still call it that, even though, like the American Pioneers, we've largely forced the natives off their land…

---

[3] It's all right if you don't get this reference. What's not all right is continuing in ignorance. *All About Eve* is one of the best movies ever made. It's about a back-stabbing, social climbing reality star. And you'll learn who Bette Davis is and why **Kim Carnes**[4] wrote that song about her.

[4] Kim Carnes is a singer and songwriter. Her most popular song was called "Bette Davis Eyes." You should listen to the song. You have no choice at this point but to watch the video. It appears to be set at a medieval-themed dinner theater, without the **gibbeting**[5].

[5] Gibbeting: to execute by hanging, or hold up for ridicule. Example, "Poor Eustace is gibbeted in the *Times* for his **atramentous**[6] chateaubriand."

[6] Find a four-year-old and ask them to show you how to use the Google.

what are you wearing?

What follows is our favorite Lawrenceville Progressive Dinner story on dressing and decorum. Printed with permission from Ron Donoughe, plein air painter extraordinaire.

He attended one of the first few progressive dinners. About 25 years ago. He'd been working all day. It was summer. He arrived wearing a nice shirt and shorts. It was hot, so he wore shorts.

When he gets there, he's the first to arrive. The hostess, apparently alone in the house, politely asks him to take a seat in the living room. He waits, a little uncomfortable. A little nervous. Then he hears the hostess shout up to the host who is upstairs:

"Honey, people are arriving."

The host shouted back, "OK! I'm just changing clothes!"

She looked at me and tsk-tsk'ed, then shouted back upstairs to her husband.

"People are arriving. Hurry up! You look fine!"

"No way!"

"What's the matter?"

"I'm wearing shorts! Only a jagoff wears shorts to the progressive dinner!"[1]

So do you need a dress code? It really depends. Do you care what people look like on the outside, or is it what's inside a person's heart that matters? You could always invite guests to dress up, as inspired by a fun theme (glam rock, beach party) or historical period (the roaring twenties, the disco 70s, post apocalyptic zombie wasteland). The authors recommend saving such shenanigans for a later iteration of the dinner – like maybe the 5th anniversary... or never.

Jag·off
noun
an American English slang term from Pittsburgh English meaning a person who is stupid or inept. It is most prominent in the Pittsburgh and Western Pennsylvania areas.

"I will now give a few words of advice to guests; puerile it may be, but which it is well to listen to, and observe. It is ridiculous to make a display of your napkin; to attach it with pins upon your bosom; to use a fork in eating soup; and to pour your coffee into the saucer to cool."
— *The Gentleman and Lady's Book of Politeness and Propriety of Deportment, Dedicated to the Youth of Both Sexes.*

Isaly's
SKYSCRAPER
CONE

Desserts

Pittsburgh FAQs

Q. Hey, you mentioned your neighborhood is called Lawrenceville. Are there any quirky, fun-loving, hipster-inspired monikers with which we could also refer to your 'hood?
A. No.

Q. Really? Cause I heard someone call it "Larryville."
A. Watch your lip or yinz gonna get your car keyed.

Q. What's "car keying?"
A. *noun, informal*
A punishment or fate that someone deserves. Also see "comeuppance."

Q. How can I inspire my neighbors to help out with dinner?
A. "Hey, yinz – this corn needs shucked."

Q. I'm new to Pittsburgh, should I serve wine and beer?
A. We refer to water as "Nature's Champagne."

Q. But, seriously, wine and beer?
A. The question you're trying to ask is: "What kind of wine should I serve with the beer that I'm obviously serving because no self-respecting Pittsburgher throws a party without beer." Please don't ask this again.

Q. Can I put out a parking chair to reserve a parking spot outside my house?
A. I don't know, can you solve the Palestinian/Israeli conflict?

Q. What's this ubiquitous "Parking Chair?"
A. See "Car Keying."

Q. Why do people hate cyclists so much?
A. Time slows down inside the confines of a car causing people to experience 5-second delays as years of their lives. Also, people are solipsistic, small-minded monsters.

Q. Pittsburgh winters are really hard.
A. That isn't a question.

Q. Pittsburgh winters are really hard?
A. Yes.

Q. I'm a POC and I noticed that Pittsburgh seems very white.
A. Welcome! You are so smart and observant! This is a work-in-progress. Please don't move back to New Jersey, New York, L.A., San Francisco, Berlin, Atlanta or Chicago. Pittsburgh needs you.

Q. People are always talking about fries on sandwiches and salads. Why do Pittsburghers put fries on sandwiches and salads?
A. "Judge a man by his questions rather than his answers." — Voltaire

Q. Hey, I noticed Carnegie Mellon University Robotics, Uber and Google are all located in Pittsburgh. It seems Pittsburgh has really become a technology hub. What are they working on?
A. A car that will drive itself to Primanti's.

Q. What is "dahntahn?"
A. Downtown.

Q. How should I pronounce "flowers?"
A. "Flyers."

Q. Can you please translate this phrase: "The will iz rill rahnd."
A. The wheel is very round.

Q. Who puts the "fun" in "Funicular?"
A. Pittsburgh!

BONUS QUESTION:
Q. You provided your film *Progression* free with this cookbook, but it isn't rated. Why?

A. We didn't want to crowdfund the $3000 dollars it would take to get the MPAA to tell us there are no boobs or female objectification or murder in our film, but nonetheless it has to be rated at least an "R" because it contains three nude male butts and words like "fucking."

Lynn Lewandowski's Rules for Progressive Dinners

Hosts

☐ Don't be nervous. Do as much ahead as you can so you can enjoy yourself.

☐ Clean the parts of the house folks will see, hide the junk, put your cats and dogs in a bedroom or out side until the course is over.

☐ Pace yourself or refrain from drinking until the course you are hosting is over. Or...learn the hard way ;)

☐ Make new recipes once or twice so you know what you are doing.

☐ One pot dishes (lasagna, casseroles, crockpot or stove top stews, soups, big bowl of salad) are easy on the host.

☐ Wine AND beer please. And also some nice sparkling water.

Guests

☐ Be polite and eat everything served. Don't be picky, just eat it — it won't kill you.

☐ Try to arrive on time. Not late, not early.

☐ Don't leave too early to get to the next course, even if it is yours. There is plenty of time to get where you need to go.

☐ When the course is over, leave, don't linger. Every one, including the host, has to get moving.

☐ Volunteer to organize it one year. It will give you an appreciation of the event. You will become a better host and guest as a result. Or not.

Conversation starters for making friends in Pittsburgh

- ☐ I love sports.
- ☐ I hate sports.
- ☐ Remember when everything was covered in a thick layer of soot?
- ☐ I love/hate bicycles.
- ☐ People today.
- ☐ Why your neighborhood is the best.
- ☐ Fries on top of other food items.
- ☐ What happened to the Hill.
- ☐ Medical marijuana.
- ☐ Healthcare.
- ☐ Universities.
- ☐ Why gender inequality and racism still exist and what action you can take to combat them.
- ☐ How pretty everyone looks.

"My advice to anyone hosting a course would be to keep it within your means. It is no time to try something new but prepare your specialty, something you are familiar with so that you can enjoy the entire event without worrying... it really doesn't matter if everything is PERFECT."
— LUPS veteran, Susan Banahasky

Recipes

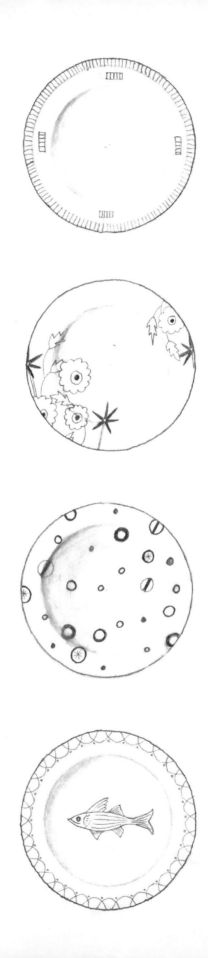

Dear Reader:

What follows is a collection of recipes donated by denizens of Lawrenceville – perpetrators of the LUPS progressive dinner, restaurateurs who operate in the neighborhood and friends of the film. They are not organized according to dining courses, but rather the courses of the heart. There are recipes to accompany friend-making, and while Homer Simpson famously told us, "You don't win friends with salad," we're certain he never sampled Michele Viola's "Sunny Mediterranean," sure to inspire the kind of bonhomie felt by Cole Porter and his beard-of-a-wife Linda Lee Thomas towards their house guests on the Riviera. If keeping old friends is your goal, you can't go wrong with Susan Banahasky's "We'll Always Have Paris." If you're in the midst of a break up and can't decide what to serve as a last meal, we offer you "Kiss My Grits," Lynn Lewandowski's cheesy and comforting reminder of the good times you spent together.

recipes for making new friends

CIAO CHOW
Sunny Mediterranean Salad
donated by Michele Viola
Serves 12

Ingredients
Olive oil
2 cloves garlic, minced
2 cups bread, cubed
Salt and pepper to taste
Generous handful assorted pitted olives, cured and calamata, especially in oil
3 good sized romaine hearts

1 cup feta or gorgonzola cheese crumbles

A few slices of fresh red onion (optional)

Chopped or grape tomatoes (optional)
1 or 2 lemons
Fresh basil or mint

Method

Wash and chop romaine hearts. Top with olives, croutons and cheese. Drizzle olive oil over the romaine hearts and topping. With a citrus reamer, add the juice of 1 or 2 fresh lemons. Add salt and pepper to taste. Sprinkle fresh herbs over top. Toss to coat all ingredients well. Let stand about 15 minutes for croutons to absorb some of the dressing.

Homemade croutons:

Pre-heat oven to 300. Pour about 1/4 cup olive oil into a large metal bowl. Add minced garlic and stir to coat sides of bowl. Add bread cubes, salt and pepper and toss until coated. Arrange bread cubes on baking sheet and bake, stirring occasionally, for about 10 minutes until croutons are golden brown.

Serve immediately.

THAT'S WHY THE LADY AND THE TRAMP

Spaghetti Carbonara
donated by Justin Severino, Chef at Cure and Morcilla

Ingredients
3 ounces fresh spaghetti
2 tablespoons salty pork bits*
2 teaspoon roasted garlic
1 tablespoon soffrito*
8 ounces vegetable stock
½ cup green peas, blanched
¼ cup pecorino romano
1 egg, whipped
Olive oil

Chives

*salty pork bits are all the odds and ends from our dry cured salumi that we can't slice that we then pulse in a food processor

*soffrito is onions slowly roasted in olive oil and salt until the onions become sweet and caramelized

(cont'd)

(continued from previous page)

Method

In a small sauce pot over medium heat start by rendering the salty pork bits until they start to become crispy, then add the roasted garlic. Fry the garlic in the fat rendered from the pork bits to develop a deeper, richer flavor. Add the soffrito and stir it into the garlic and crispy pork bits. Add the vegetable stock and peas to the sauce pot and bring to just under a simmer. Cook the spaghetti in boiling salted water for 1 minute. Pull the cooked spaghetti directly from the boiling water into the sauce pot. Add half of the pecorino, reserving the other half for garnish. While constantly stirring over medium heat, add the whipped eggs using a squirt bottle. Continue to cook and stir until sauce begins to thicken. Transfer immediately to a bowl and garnish with the remaining pecorino romano, olive oil and chives.

PEE SOUP

Butternut Squash Apple Cider Soup
(as seen in *Progression*)

Ingredients

½ cup butter

1 medium-large butternut squash, halved, seeded and chopped into 1-inch cubes

2 cups leeks, chopped (white and pale green parts only)

2 carrots, peeled and chopped

2 celery stalks, chopped

2 small apples, peeled and chopped

1-½ teaspoons dried thyme

½ teaspoon crumbled dried sage leaves

5 cups chicken stock or vegetable stock

1-½ cups apple cider

2/3 cup sour cream

½ cup whipping cream

Fresh chives, chopped

Method

Soup and cider cream can be made 1 day ahead.
Cover separately and refrigerate.

To prepare soup:
Melt butter in heavy large saucepan over medium-high heat. Add squash, leeks, carrot and celery;
sauté until slightly softened, about 15 minutes. Mix
in apples, thyme and sage. Add stock and 1 cup cider
and bring to boil. Reduce heat to medium-low. Cover
and simmer until apples are tender, 20-30 minutes.
Working in batches, purée soup in blender. Return
blended soup to pan.

To prepare cider cream:
Reduce remaining 1/2 cup cider in heavy small
saucepan by boiling for about 5 minutes. Cool. Place
sour cream in small bowl. Whisk in reduced cider.

To serve:
Bring soup to simmer. Mix in whipping cream. Ladle
soup into bowls. Drizzle with cider cream. Top with
chives.

recipes for keeping old friends

WE'LL ALWAYS HAVE PARIS

Moroccan Chicken with Figs and Couscous
donated by Susan Banahasky

Serves 4

Ingredients
2 tablespoons olive oil
2 medium cloves garlic, peeled and minced
6 skinless, boneless chicken thighs cut into quarters
1-½ teaspoons ground cumin
½ teaspoon ground ginger
¼ teaspoon cayenne pepper
1/8 teaspoon turmeric
1 medium red onion, quartered and thinly sliced
½ cup chicken broth
1 cinnamon stick
10 dried figs, cut into quarters
¼ cup golden raisins
¼ cup garbanzo beans
1 tablespoon honey
½ teaspoon sesame oil
¼ teaspoon salt
Freshly ground black pepper to taste
1 tablespoon chopped cilantro or parsley

Couscous:
¾ cup chicken broth
1-¼ cups water
¼ teaspoon salt

1 cup uncooked couscous

Method

To prepare the chicken:
Pour olive oil into a large skillet over medium heat. When hot, add the garlic and sauté 1 minute. Then add the chicken, cumin, ginger, cayenne and turmeric. Sauté 3 minutes. Remove the chicken from the pan.

Put the onion into the pan with about a tablespoon of the broth and sauté 5 minutes. Put the chicken back into the pan. Add the remaining broth, cinnamon stick, figs, raisins, garbanzo beans, honey, sesame oil, salt and pepper. Cover and simmer over medium-low heat 20 minutes, or until the chicken is cooked through.

To prepare the couscous:
In a medium-size pan combine the chicken broth, water, salt and couscous. Bring to a boil, stirring well. Remove from the heat and set aside 5 minutes.

To serve:
Stir cilantro into the chicken. Fluff couscous with a fork and transfer to plates. Spoon chicken over the couscous and serve.

THEY DANCE BY THE LIGHT OF THE MOON

Hoot Night Veggie Rice
donated by Sherrie Flick

Ingredients

2 tablespoons olive oil

3-6 garlic cloves, chopped

6 medium-sized cremini mushrooms, sliced

12 whole pea pods, with the ends snapped off

6 large kale leaves, with the green zippered off the stem and chopped into thin strips

1-2 cups cooked brown rice that you already have in your fridge

2 tablespoons pesto that you've made from foraged ramps and parsley that overwintered in your yard — or any pesto

Salt

Pepper

Method

First. You need friends to play music with. You call the nights you meet up to play hoot nights. Next, work in the garden far too late into the day. Realize that you have a half hour to make food for the hoot potluck. Heat a large cast iron skillet (or any comparable pan) at medium heat. Add the 2 tablespoons olive oil. Add the chopped garlic—just as it begins to smell garlicky (less than a minute — do not burn the garlic), add the sliced mushrooms. Sauté them until they begin to sweat their juices. You'll think they're done, but they're not—wait for the juices. It's worth it. Next add the pea pods. Sauté for 2 minutes, add the chopped kale—ideally water still clings to the leaves. This water will help steam cook the kale in your pan. This is when I add salt and pepper, to taste. Once the kale wilts, add your cooked brown rice (or any grain that you had the foresight to make and not finish). Stir. Add the pesto. Stir. Tap the wooden spoon on the side of the pan. Done. Package it up, get your instrument—grab that bottle of wine—and go.

WHAT I DID WITH THE FUCKING SHALLOTS

Easy Green Salad With Shallots
(as seen in *Progression*)

Ingredients
1 head bibb lettuce
1 medium shallot
14-ounce jar hearts of palm
1 shaved carrot
2 lemons
1 clove garlic
2 tablespoons olive oil
Salt to taste
Fresh ground pepper

Method

Dice garlic and shallots. Macerate them by combining in small dish with juice of 2 lemons. Set aside for 10 minutes.

Clean lettuce, tear into smaller pieces. Shave carrots. Slice hearts of palm into chunks about the size of a stack of four nickels.

Plate the lettuce. Sprinkle carrots and hearts of palm.

Combine olive oil, lemon juice, shallots, garlic and salt. Shake or stir dressing. Dress salads. Add fresh ground pepper to taste.

break up meals

KISS MY GRITS

Grits and Roasted Vegetables
donated by Lynn Lewandowski

Ingredients
1 package grits
1 cup half-and-half
8 ounces sharp white cheddar, shredded
Yellow bell pepper
Red bell pepper
Orange bell pepper
Medium zucchini
Small eggplant
20 cherry tomatoes
2 tablespoons olive oil
Salt & pepper to taste
Small jar capers
½ cup pesto
Splash balsamic vinegar

Method

Grits:
Prepare grits (Trader Joe's are good) according to package directions, but instead of using milk at the end, use half and half and double it. You want the grits to be loose and creamy. Add either sharp white cheddar or an Italian cheese blend (again, Trader Joe's Quattro Formaggio is good for this), reserving a handful to sprinkle on top before baking. After grits are cooked and cheese has been added, spoon into shallow oven-safe dishes and level, leaving room for vegetables. Set aside.

Roasted Vegetables:
Preheat oven to 400 degrees. Slice three colors of sweet peppers, eggplant, and zucchini into bite-sized pieces. Add halved cherry tomatoes. Coat vegetables with good olive oil, a little salt and coarsely ground pepper. Spread in a shallow ceramic baking dish and roast in 400 degree oven, turning once or twice, until caramelized and soft, about 30 minutes.

Scrape roasted veggies into a large bowl and add capers, pesto and a splash of balsamic vinegar. Stir until veggies are coated.

Spoon veggie mixture on top of the grits, sprinkle with remaining cheese and bake at 350 degrees until cheese melts and grits are heated through.

This recipe is great when made ahead of time, refrigerated and reheated.

LET'S KEEP IT CHILL

Watermelon Gazpacho
donated by Yvette Benhamou, Tender Bar+Kitchen

Ingredients
6 cups watermelon, cubed
2 cucumbers, diced
2 red bell peppers, diced
1 large shallot, minced
½ jalapeno pepper, minced
¼ cup lemon juice
2 tablespoons extra virgin olive oil
3 tablespoons fresh mint, finely chopped
2 tablespoons fresh ginger, minced
3 tablespoons agave nectar
½ cup pineapple juice
Fresh mint leaves for garnish

Method

Reserve 20 small pieces of watermelon for garnish. Working in batches, place the remaining watermelon, the cucumbers, red bell peppers, shallot, jalapeno pepper, lemon juice, olive oil, chopped fresh mint, ginger, agave, and pineapple juice into a blender, and blend for about 15 seconds per batch. The mixture should be well blended but retain some texture. Pour into a large pitcher or bowl and refrigerate 1 hour.

Serve in bowls, and garnish each bowl with a couple of chunks of the retained watermelon and 2 small mint leaves. (And maybe a dollop of yogurt.)

HASTA LA VISTA, BABY

Chicken Enchilada Casserole
donated by Meals with Maya

Ingredients
12 6-inch corn tortillas
1-½ pounds boneless chicken breasts or 1 roast chicken, shredded
4 cups shredded mozzarella
2 12-ounce jars tomatillo salsa

Optional Garnish:
Chopped avocado, cilantro, jalapeno
Sour cream or greek yogurt
Red or green salsa

Method

Poach chicken breasts in salted water (reserve poaching liquid), cool and then shred (if not using roast chicken). Shred poached chicken by hand or save time by using a stand mixer or beaters. Pour one-half jar salsa in the bottom of a glass 9x13" baking dish. Lay 6 tortillas over bottom of pan. Spread half the shredded chicken over the tortillas, then half the shredded cheese. Fill up the half-full salsa jar with poaching liquid or water, shake up and pour over chicken and cheese. Layer remaining 6 tortillas, top with remaining chicken. Pour over another half jar of salsa. Fill up jar with poaching liquid or water, shake to incorporate and then pour over the casserole. Casserole can be frozen, wrapped tightly in plastic wrap, or kept in fridge to bake later in the week.

Baking

Cover with foil and bake 1 hour at 375 degrees. Uncover, top with remaining cheese and bake 15 minutes more until cheese is melted and browned. Serve topped with any optional garnishes.

Make it Vegetarian

Replace the chicken with 2 cans of black beans and a cup of frozen corn, or your choice of add-ins below.

Add Sneaky Vegetables

If you have time, before layering the casserole, blend your salsa with some spinach and/or leftover broccoli stems (or really any green things you have lying around). Add the chicken stock or water to the blender at the end and process.

(cont'd)

(continued from previous page)

Add-ins

Layer in any of these ingredients along with the chicken to bulk up this casserole:

Thinly sliced raw sweet potatoes
Leftover roasted sweet potatoes
Sliced jalapeno
Chopped scallions
Chopped fresh cilantro

Recipe inspired by Layered Chicken Enchiladas with Tomatillo Cilantro Sauce from *Bon Appetit*, September 2005.

SMELL THE CRIES

Roasted Leg of Lamb with Cherries
(as seen in *Progression*)

Ingredients
5 pound leg of lamb
4 cloves garlic, sliced
2 tablespoons fresh rosemary
Salt
Ground black pepper
½ cup butter
2 shallots, minced
2 cups cherries, pitted and halved
¾ cup red wine
1 tablespoon orange zest, finely shredded
1 tablespoon sugar
2 tablespoons fresh lemon juice

Method

Lamb:

Preheat oven to 350 degrees F (175 degrees C). Cut slits in the top of the leg of lamb every 3 to 4 inches, push slices of garlic through slits down into the meat. Set aside 1 tablespoon butter for the cherry sauce. Rub lamb with remaining butter. Salt and pepper generously all over the top of lamb. Place several sprigs of fresh rosemary under and on top of the lamb. Place lamb on roasting pan. Roast in preheated oven until the lamb is cooked to desired doneness, about 1-¾ to 2 hours. Do not overcook the lamb; the flavor is best if meat is still slightly pink. Let rest at least 10 minutes before carving. For medium-rare to medium doneness, an instant-read thermometer inserted into the center should read at least 135 degrees. The meat will continue to cook slightly after it is removed from the oven.

Cherry Sauce:

Melt one tablespoon butter in a saucepan and sauté shallots over medium heat until soft, about 3 minutes. Add cherries and stir 2 minutes. Add red wine, orange zest, sugar, lemon juice, and a pinch of salt. Cook, stirring often, until liquid reduces by half. Let cool slightly. Serve warm alongside the lamb.

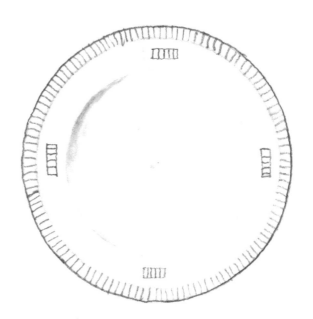

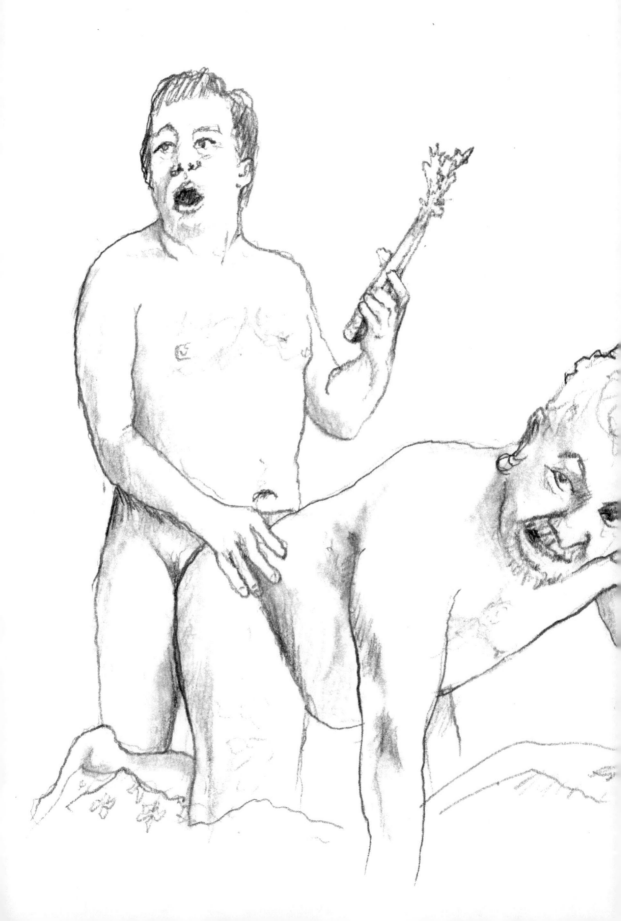

recipes for getting sexy

SOMETIMES A CIGAR ISN'T JUST A CIGAR

Apricot/Feta Cigars
donated by Mary M. Mazziotti

Ingredients
1 pound feta cheese
1 egg
½ cup plain yogurt
Handful dried apricots
Package square wonton wrappers

Method

Get about a pound of feta cheese (if you live in Pittsburgh, you're lucky because you can get it at Salonika in the Strip District — good quality & good price). Mash it up with one egg and some plain yogurt, maybe 1/2 cup or so. Chop up a handful of dried apricots. Actually, don't chop them. Cut them into little pieces with scissors. It's much easier. Mix them into the feta well.

Now open a package of square wonton wrappers. Put a dollop of filling in a wrapper, fold the ends over a bit and roll it up like a little cigar. Put these on a greased baking sheet and stick them into a 350 degree oven until they are golden brown, I don't know, say about 10-12 minutes.

Let them cool down a bit, but they are best served warm. Crunch, salty and sweet! People really like these.

HOT DATES

Hot Dates (who doesn't like these?)
donated by Garry Pyles

Ingredients
20 pitted dates
10 ounces aged manchego cheese
Bunch fresh mint leaves
10 ounces pancetta, thinly sliced

Method

If you are fortunate enough to live in Pittsburgh, head on down to Penn Mac in the Strip for everything you need. "Dear Heart" at the cheese counter will hook you up with a great block of manchego and the guys at the meat counter will slice your pancetta for you nice and thin. Find dates with the dried fruits. Once you get everything, here is what you do:

Slice manchego into small wedge-shaped pieces. Wrap the cheese with a mint leaf. Push wrapped cheese into the date. Don't worry if it breaks open. Wrap stuffed date with a slice of pancetta. Arrange on baking sheet and bake in 350 degree oven until pancetta is crisp, about 20 minutes. Serve with chopped mint sprinkled over them.

A SWEET TART

Apple Tart Cake
donated by Chuck and Danielle Staresinic

This is a professional-looking dessert. The Granny Smith apples differentiate this tart from all others.

Ingredients
¾ cup granulated sugar (I tried Blue Agave and it
    works, use less, ½ cup)
1 cup all-purpose flour
1 teaspoon baking powder
8 tablespoons cold unsalted butter,
    cut in a few pieces
1 teaspoon vanilla extract
1 large egg, lightly beaten

2-3 large Granny Smith apples, peeled, cored, thinly sliced (I like the skin on and it worked for me)
3 tablespoons granulated sugar
1 teaspoon ground cinnamon
1 large egg

Method

Preheat oven to 350. Butter & flour 9-inch spring-form pan.

Combine sugar, flour and baking powder in food processor fitted with steel blade. Pulse. Set aside 3 tablespoons butter for the topping. Add 5 tablespoons butter, to food processor and pulse until there are no large lumps. Add vanilla and egg, pulse several times only until it resembles cornmeal (note if you pulse too much, it forms a ball that is difficult to work with). Dump into springform pan, distribute evenly with fingertips, then gently press down and make a slight rim at the edge (don't press it too hard). Arrange apple slices on top in tight circular pattern. Really squeeze them in. Place in oven, bake for 40 minutes.

Melt remaining 2 tablespoons butter and let cool slightly. Combine granulated sugar, melted butter, cinnamon and egg in a small bowl and blend well. After cake has baked for 40 minutes, remove it and spoon the topping evenly over the top. Bake for another 20 minutes, until the topping looks set. Remove from oven and cool 20 minutes on a wire rack. Then, run thin knife around edge to release any stuck areas and remove side of spring pan. Cool completely before serving. It is good with vanilla or coffee or caramel ice cream. If possible, make a day ahead and wrap in plastic, as it is better on the second day.

Note: If your oven runs hot, reduce the temperature because the base of the cake could burn before the apples are fully cooked.

ADD YOUR OWN SAUSAGE

Better Than Any of Them Restaurant Pierogies
(as seen in *Progression*)

Ingredients
2 cups flour
½ teaspoon salt
1 large egg
½ cup sour cream
¼ cup butter, softened and cut into small pieces
Butter and onions for sautéing
5 large potatoes
Large onion, finely chopped
4 tablespoons butter
4-8 ounces cheddar cheese, grated
Salt and pepper to taste
Large onion, coarsely chopped

Method

Pierogi Dough:

To prepare the pierogi dough, mix together the flour
and salt. Beat the egg, then add all at once to the
flour mixture. Add sour cream and the softened butter
pieces and work until the dough loses most of its
stickiness (about 5-7 minutes). You can use a food
processor with a dough hook for this, but be careful
not to overbeat. Wrap the dough in plastic and refrigerate for 20-30 minutes or overnight. The dough can
be kept in the refrigerator for up to 2 days. Each batch
of dough makes about 12-15 pierogies, depending on
size.

Potato, Cheese and Onion Filling:

Peel and boil 5 large potatoes until soft. While the potatoes are boiling, finely chop 1 large onion and sauté in 2 tablespoons butter until soft and translucent. Mash the potatoes with the sautéed onions and 4-8 ounces of grated cheddar cheese (depending on how cheesy you want your pierogies), adding salt and pepper to taste. You can also add some fresh parsley, bacon bits, chives, or other enhancements if you desire. Let the potato mixture cool and then form into 1-inch balls.

Prepare the Pierogies:

Roll the pierogi dough on a floured board or countertop until 1/8" thick. Cut circles of dough (2" for small pierogies and 3-3 1/2" for large pierogies) with a cookie cutter or drinking glass. Place a small ball of filling (about a tablespoon) on each dough round and fold the dough over, forming a semi-circle. Press the edges together with the tines of a fork. Boil the pierogies a few at a time in a large pot of water. They are done when they float to the top (about 8-10 minutes). Rinse in cool water and let dry. Coarsely chop 1 large onion then sauté in 2 tablespoons butter in a large pan until soft. Then add pierogies and pan fry until lightly crispy.

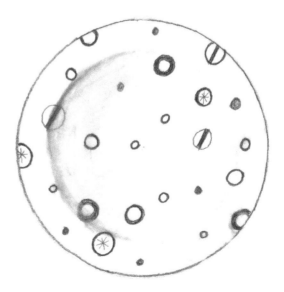

recipes for the pregnant or other special guests

FOR ALL MY HONIES

Whole Wheat Orange Cardamom Honey Cake with Honey Candied Oranges & Whipped Cream Featuring Wigle Whiskey Landlocked Spiced Distilled Mead donated by Quelcy Kogel

About This Recipe:

This recipe starts by candying oranges with honey, instead of the traditional sugar approach, which yields a more complex flavor. The remaining syrup finds its way into each element of the dessert. Add a tablespoon or two to the whipped cream, and use the remaining syrup to seep into the cake when it's fresh from the oven. Be sure to use a local, raw honey for the most flavor and to support your local beekeepers. If you're not in Wigle's shipping range, you can road trip to Pittsburgh, or substitute your favorite rum or mead. For a simple cocktail, add one of the honey candied orange slices to a glass of Landlocked Spiced on the rocks, and sip slowly.

Honey Candied Oranges & Syrup
Ingredients
¾ cup local, raw honey
¼ cup fresh-squeezed orange juice
1/3 cup lemon juice (from 2 organic lemons)
¼ cup Wigle Landlocked Spiced
2 oranges, sliced 1/4-inch thick

Method

In large skillet, combine honey, orange juice, lemon juice and Landlocked. Bring to a boil. Add orange slices. Simmer 10 to 15 minutes, until oranges are translucent. Remove slices from syrup and cool completely. Reserve orange syrup.

Orange Honey Whipped Cream
Ingredients
1 cup organic heavy cream, chilled
1 teaspoon pure vanilla extract
2-3 tablespoons orange syrup
1-2 tablespoons Wigle Landlocked Spiced, to taste (optional)

Method

In the chilled bowl of a stand mixer, combine the heavy cream, vanilla and orange syrup. Beat on medium high until soft peaks form. Add Landlocked Spiced, and beat until incorporated. Keep chilled until ready to use.

Whole Wheat Orange Cardamom Honey Cake
Ingredients
2 cups organic whole-wheat pastry flour
1 teaspoon baking powder
½ teaspoon baking soda
¼ teaspoon salt
1-½ teaspoon ground cardamom
8 tablespoons organic, unsalted butter, softened, plus more for greasing pan
½ cup local, raw, wildflower honey
(cont'd)

(continued from previous page)

Zest of 1 organic orange
½ teaspoon pure vanilla extract
2 eggs (organic/cage-free)
¾ cup organic, plain, full-fat Greek yogurt

Method
Preheat oven to 350. Butter a 9-inch springform pan. In a medium bowl, whisk together flour, baking powder, baking soda, salt, and cardamom. Set aside.

With an electric mixer, beat the butter until light and fluffy, about 1 minute. Add honey and beat until well incorporated, about 1 minute. Add the orange zest and vanilla, then add the eggs, one at a time, mixing until well-incorporated. Add half of the dry ingredients, stir until just combined. Add the yogurt, stir. Add the remaining dry ingredients and stir until just combined.

Spread the batter evenly into the prepared pan and bake until a tester comes out clean, about 35 minutes. Transfer cake to a cooling rack. Use a cake tester or a skewer to poke holes in the surface of the cake. Pour remaining Honey Orange Syrup over the cake.

Allow to cool completely, and then top with whipped cream and candied orange slices.

Enjoy!

IT'S COMPLICATED

Roasted Butternut Squash Lasagna
donated by Lynn Lewandowski

Ingredients
1 large butternut squash
Olive oil
Salt
Freshly ground pepper
2-½ cups milk, heated
Sprig rosemary or thyme
1 clove garlic
4 tablespoons butter
4 tablespoons flour
Grated nutmeg
2 cups gruyere or aged gouda cheese, shredded
2 large onions, sliced
Pinch sugar
Splash white wine or brandy
1 package no-boil lasagna noodles

Method

Peel, halve, seed and cut butternut squash into thick slices, about 2-3 inches long. Toss in a bowl with olive oil, salt and pepper. Spread onto a rimmed cookie sheet, lined with parchment paper. Use two if needed so that the squash is not crowded. Roast in a preheated 400 degree oven for about 30 minutes, turning once or twice, until edges start to caramelize and pieces of squash soften.

To make a basic béchamel sauce, gently heat the milk with a sprig of rosemary or thyme, and a clove of garlic. Let steep on low heat for 10 minutes, then remove from heat, let the milk rest until cool, and remove the herbs and garlic. Heat milk again, but don't let it boil. In a separate, heavy-bottomed saucepan, melt the butter. Stirring constantly, add the flour and cook until a paste forms and bubbles. Do not allow it to brown. Now add the hot milk, continuing to stir as the sauce thickens. Bring it to a boil. Add salt and pepper to taste, lower the heat, and cook, stirring for 2 to 3 minutes more. Remove from heat. Add grated nutmeg and coarsely ground pepper to taste, and about one cup of shredded gruyere or aged gouda cheese. Add salt if needed.

Caramelize two sliced large onions in olive oil, a little butter, pepper, salt and a sprinkle of sugar. The onions should become soft and nicely browned, but not burnt. This takes a while, so keep the heat low to medium, and stir occasionally. Add a splash of white wine or even brandy if you wish.

Preheat oven to 350 degrees. Layer the ingredients in a ceramic casserole or lasagna pan in this order: bechamel sauce, no-boil lasagna noodles, butternut squash, onions.

Use three layers of noodles, with béchamel and the remaining gruyere or gouda cheese on top. Loosely cover with foil. Bake for about 30 minutes, uncover, and bake until top starts to brown, about 10 more minutes. Cool before cutting and serving.

*This can be made ahead and reheated. Or the components can be made ahead and assembled and baked before serving.

WE'RE HERE, WE'RE VEGAN, GET USED TO IT!

Chilled Beet Soup
donated by Kyle Bostian

Ingredients
4-6 beets
4-6 new potatoes
3 cloves garlic, diced
Large sweet onion, chopped
Lemon
½ cup vegetable broth (use milk for non-vegan)
Dill
Tarragon
Sea salt

Cayenne pepper (optional)

Method

Place bunch of beets (greens/stems removed but skins still on) in pot of water, bring to boil, and cook 30-35 minutes. Rinse/soak in cold water. Once cool enough to handle, remove skins (they should slide right off) and chop beets into chunks. Chop roughly the same volume of new potatoes (skins still on) and place in pot of water, bring to boil, and cook 10-15 minutes. Rinse with cold water and drain.

Combine beets and potatoes in food processor. Add diced garlic (anywhere from one to several cloves), chopped sweet onion (medium to large), and lemon juice (start with half a lemon, more to taste). Add a little broth and puree, adding splashes of broth until mixture reaches desired consistency. During the pureeing process, season with the following ingredients (amounts to taste, but listed from what's likely the greatest to smallest quantity): dill, tarragon, sea salt, cayenne pepper (optional).

Transfer mixture to a large bowl, cover and refrigerate for at least several hours (better overnight). Enjoy!

THESE FLYERS ARE EDIBLE

Arugula Salad with Duck Confit,
Prawned Apple Chips and Edible Flowers
(as seen in *Progression*)

Serves 6

Ingredients
4 duck legs
Golden delicious apple
1 bunch arugula (about 4 ounces)
2 cloves garlic, minced
¼ cup red onion, finely chopped
1 lemon
¼ cup olive oil
Edible flowers (some examples: lavender, thyme, dill,cilantro, day lily, squash blossom, nasturtiums, chives, and basil)

Method

Duck Confit:
Preheat oven to 350. Place duck legs, fat side down, in a large ovenproof skillet. To render fat, cook over medium-high heat for about 20 minutes. When there is ¼ inch of rendered fat in the pan, turn duck legs over, cover the pan, and place in the oven. Roast for 2 hours, then remove cover and continue roasting for one hour or more until duck is golden brown. Remove from oven and let cool for 20 minutes. When duck is still warm, remove the meat from the bones, discarding bits of bone or gristle. Shred the meat, using two forks or your fingers, or leave it in larger chunks if you prefer.

Dried Apple Chips:
Preheat oven to 225 degrees. Lay apple on side and slice into ¼-inch round rings. Remove seeds. Arrange apples rings on a metal baking sheet. Bake in the pre-heated oven until apples are dried and edges curl up, 45 minutes to 1 hour. Remove from oven and transfer slices to a wire rack until cooled and crispy. Set aside.

Dressing:
Combine minced garlic and finely chopped red onion. Macerate them by combining in small dish with juice of 1 lemon. Set aside for 10 minutes. Then combine olive oil, lemon juice, garlic red onion and salt. Shake or stir dressing.

Shred arugula into large bowl, and toss with dressing. Plate arugula and top with duck confit, edible flowers. Slit apple ring and twist into prawn shape. Place prawned apple chip on top of center of salad, and serve.

appendix

Draw a DIAGRAM of host locations, with numbered slots for each location's guest capacity. Now, you begin the process of assigning participants to each course.

Here's where the organizing gets really interesting. Once you have your diagram of host locations you can start filling in seats.

~Diagram~

Soup:	Salad:	Entreé:
Location 1	**Location 1**	**Location 1**
Address:	Address:	Address:
Guests	Guests	Guests
1. 5.	1. 5.	1. 5.
2. 6.	2. 6.	2. 6.
3. 7.	3. 7.	3. 7.
4. 8.	4. 8.	4. 8.
Location 2	**Location 2**	**Location 2**
Address:	Address:	Address:
Guests	Guests	Guests
1. 5	1. 5.	1. 5.
2. 6	2. 6.	2. 6.
3. 7.	3. 7.	3. 7.
4. 8.	4. 8.	4. 8.
Location 3	**Location 3**	**Location 3**
Address:	Address:	Address:
Guests	Guests	Guests
1. 5	1. 5.	1. 5.
2. 6.	2. 6.	2. 6.
3. 7.	3. 7.	3. 7.
4. 8.	4. 8.	4. 8.

Each attendee or couple at the progressive dinner gets a dance card that tells them where to go next after each course. It's handy, easy to read, and a nice keepsake after the event. Print 'em up, fill 'em out using your handy dandy DIAGRAM as your guide. Distribute them at the Appetizer course.

Dance Card

Your soup will be served at: _____

Your salad will be served at: _____

Your entrée will be served at: _____

Bon Appetit!

BREAD PLATE • BREAD KNIFE • DESSERT SPOON • CAKE FORK • PLACE CARD • NAPKIN • SALAD FORK • DINNER FORK • SERVICE PLATE • SALAD PLATE • DINNER KNIFE • TEASPOON • SOUP SPOON • CUP AND SAUCER • WATER GLASS • WINE GLASS (RED) • WINE GLASS (WHITE)

To redeem your
Free Copy
of the Pittsburgh feature film comedy

Progression

email us at
progressionfilm@gmail.com

Please include the subject line:
FREE COPY and this unique code: 81212FMC

Made in the USA
Charleston, SC
05 December 2016